PREHISTORIC WORLD

CRETACEOUS LIFE

Dougal Dixon

BARRON'S

First edition for the United States, its territories and dependencies, Canada, and
the Philippine Republic published in 2006 by Barron's Educational Series, Inc.

Copyright © 2006 *ticktock* Entertainment Ltd. First published in Great Britain by ticktock Media Ltd.

All inquiries should be addressed to:
Barron's Educational Series, Inc.
250 Wireless Blvd.
Hauppauge, New York 11788
www.barronseduc.com

Library of Congress Control Number: 2005938240

ISBN-13: 978-0-7641-3483-8
ISBN-10: 0-7641-3483-3

Printed in China
9 8 7 6 5 4 3 2 1

CONTENTS

INTRODUCTION

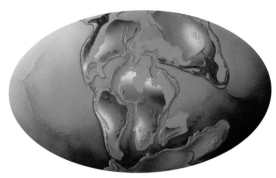

This map shows how the Earth looked in the Cretaceous Period. The continents were separate from each other, but slowly moving into the positions that we know today.

This map shows how the Earth looks today. North and South America are now joined together, and Asia is linked to Europe and Africa.

Prehistoric World is a series of six books that follows the evolution of animals.

The Earth's history is divided into sections called eras, which are then divided into periods. These last millions of years. Each book in this series looks at the most exciting animals from prehistory periods.

During the Cretaceous Period many types of dinosaurs evolved, including the most famous predator of all – *Tyrannosaurus*. Smaller, feathered creatures also evolved.

PREHISTORIC WORLD TIMELINE

Use this timeline to trace prehistoric life. **It shows how simple creatures evolved into more different kinds.** This took millions and millions of years. That is what MYA stands for – millions of years ago.

	BOOK	PERIOD	
CENOZOIC ERA	**THE ICE AGE**	1.75 MYA to now QUATERNARY	*This is a period of ice ages and mammals. Our direct relatives, Homo sapiens, also appear.*
	ANCIENT MAMMALS	65 to 1.75 MYA TERTIARY	*Giant mammals and huge hunting birds appear in this period. Our first human relatives also start to evolve.*
MESOZOIC ERA	**CRETACEOUS LIFE**	135 to 65 MYA CRETACEOUS	*Huge dinosaurs evolve. They all die by the end of this period.*
	JURASSIC LIFE	203 to 135 MYA JURASSIC	*Large and small dinosaurs and flying creatures develop.*
	TRIASSIC LIFE	250 to 203 MYA TRIASSIC	*The "Age of Dinosaurs" begins. Mammals also start to appear.*
PALEOZOIC ERA	**EARLY LIFE**	295 to 250 MYA PERMIAN	*Sail-backed reptiles start to appear.*
		355 to 295 MYA CARBONIFEROUS	*The first reptiles appear, and tropical forests develop.*
		410 to 355 MYA DEVONIAN	*Bony fish evolve. Trees and insects appear.*
		435 to 410 MYA SILURIAN	*Fish with jaws develop, and land creatures appear.*
		500 to 435 MYA ORDOVICIAN	*Primitive fishes, trilobites, shellfish, and plants evolve.*
		540 to 500 MYA CAMBRIAN	*First animals with skeletons appear.*

QUETZALCOATLUS

Toward the end of the Cretaceous era, the flying reptiles – the pterosaurs – became truly enormous. *Quetzalcoatlus* was among the biggest, and was the size of a small airplane. Despite its huge wingspan, it would not have weighed much more than an adult human.

Most pterosaurs lived near the sea, where they hunted for fish. *Quetzalcoatlus* was different; it lived far inland. It may have been a scavenger, feeding on the bodies of dinosaurs that had died on the open plains. It would have soared like a vulture and spotted dead animals from far away.

A complete skeleton of *Quetzalcoatlus* has never been found. We have a good idea of what it looked like from the few fossils that have been found and put together, like this one.

The plesiosaurs were swimming reptiles, and most had very long necks. *Elasmosaurus* had a neck that was 25 feet (7.5 meters) long – more than half of its total length. It cruised the warm waters of the shallow sea that stretched across North America at the end of the Cretaceous Period, hunting fish that were in great supply there.

The way the vertebrae of the neck are joined together suggests that *Elasmosaurus* swam near the surface of the water and reached down to catch its prey. The long neck probably also allowed it to reach out and snatch fish, without moving its body too far or too quickly.

Elasmosaurus had tiny nostrils which were not used for breathing, but to sense prey moving in the water. To breathe, *Elasmosaurus* would have swum to the surface of the sea to take in air through its mouth.

ANIMAL
FACTFILE

NAME: *Elasmosaurus* (thin plate lizard)

PRONOUNCED: eh-laz-mo-sawr-us

GROUP: Plesiosaur

WHERE IT LIVED: Kansas

WHEN IT LIVED: Late Cretaceous Period (69 to 66 million years ago)

LENGTH: 45 feet (13 meters)

SPECIAL FEATURES: Long neck with 71 vertebrae (we humans have only 7)

FOOD: Fish

MAIN ENEMY: Big swimming reptiles like *Tylosaurus*

DID YOU KNOW?: The first scientist to study *Elasmosaurus* built the skeleton wrongly. He put the head on the tail end, thinking the short tail was the neck and the long neck was the tail.

TYLOSAURUS

Tylosaurus was one of the biggest and fiercest of the mosasaurs. These were giant lizards who evolved to swim. By the Late Cretaceous Period, ichthyosaurs (the main streamlined sea hunters of the Jurassic) were extinct. The mosasaurs evolved in their place, eating the same food and hunting the same way.

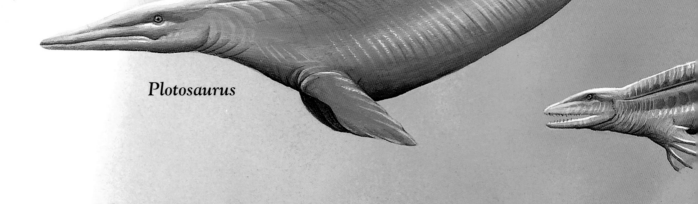

Plotosaurus

Tylosaurus

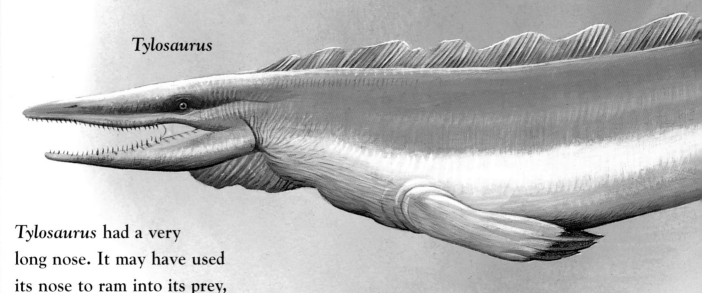

Tylosaurus had a very long nose. It may have used its nose to ram into its prey, stunning it so it could be eaten.

Pliolatecarpus

The toes of *Tylosaurus* were joined to make a paddle shape. The tail was flat and used to push the animal through the water with powerful sideways strokes.

*I*GUANODON

Iguanodon was one of the first dinosaurs to be discovered. Scientists studying its fossil thought that it looked like a big reptile. Most big reptiles are meat-eaters, but the teeth of this fossil showed it ate plants. The iguana, a plant-eating lizard, has teeth similar to *Iguanodon*. So the plant-eating dinosaur was named *Iguanodon* – "iguana tooth."

Scientists used to think that *Iguanodon* stood upright, resting on its tail like a kangaroo. Now they think that it usually walked on all fours, and only reached up to feed.

Iguanodon was common in northern Europe, but it had close relatives all over the world. *Muttaburrasaurus* lived in Australia, while big-nosed *Altirhinus* (right) lived in Mongolia.

ANIMAL FACTFILE

NAME: *Iguanodon* (iguana tooth)

PRONOUNCED: ig-wan-oh-don

GROUP: Ornithopod dinosaur

WHERE IT LIVED: Northern Europe

WHEN IT LIVED: Early Cretaceous Period (135 to 125 million years ago)

LENGTH: 30 feet (9 meters)

SPECIAL FEATURES: First finger had a big horny spike for defense, and for ripping trees

FOOD: Plants

MAIN ENEMY: Big meat-eating dinosaurs, like *Neovenator*

DID YOU KNOW?: *Iguanodon's* fifth finger was small and flexible, and used like a thumb.

 OLOROTITAN

The duckbills were one of the main plant-eaters at the end of the Cretaceous Period. They are called duckbills because their mouth looked like the beak of a duck. The beak was used to strip leaves and needles from trees. The back of the mouth had a massive set of chewing teeth that could deal with the toughest plant material.

Fossils tell us a lot about what an animal looked like and what it ate. It is much harder to work out an animal's behavior. Scientists think the duckbills lived in groups and laid their eggs in nests. Young dinosaurs would have stayed in the herd until they were adults.

The crests of the duckbills were often hollow and might have been used to make noises for signaling. Each shape of crest might have made a different noise, and so different herds could tell each other apart.

ANIMAL FACTFILE

NAME: *Olorotitan* (giant swan)

PRONOUNCED: oh-low-row-tie-tan

GROUP: Ornithopod dinosaur

WHERE IT LIVED: Russia

WHEN IT LIVED: Late Cretaceous Period (70 to 65 million years ago)

LENGTH: 30 feet (9 meters)

SPECIAL FEATURES: Strangely shaped crest on the head

FOOD: Twigs, leaves, and conifer needles

MAIN ENEMY: Big meat-eating dinosaurs like *Tyrannosaurus*

DID YOU KNOW?: *Olorotitan* was given its name because its neck was particularly long and swan-like.

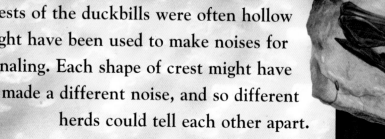

TARCHIA

The ankylosaurs were the most heavily armored group of animals to exist. Their backs were tightly packed with armor plates making them as tough as tanks. They were also armed – some with spikes that stuck out at the side and some with clubs on their tails. *Tarchia* was an ankylosaur that carried a club.

Tarchia means "brainy" and this dinosaur had a bigger brain-case than other ankylosaurs. Despite its name, it was not a very intelligent animal.

ANIMAL
FACTFILE

NAME: *Tarchia* (brainy)

PRONOUNCED: tar-chee-a

GROUP: Thyreophoran dinosaur

WHERE IT LIVED: Asia

WHEN IT LIVED: Late Cretaceous Period (78 to 69 million years ago)

LENGTH: 20 feet (6 meters)

SPECIAL FEATURES: Back covered in armor, club on the end of its tail

FOOD: Low-growing plants

MAIN ENEMY: Big meat-eating dinosaurs like *Tyrannosaurus*

DID YOU KNOW?: Vertebrae on the end of the tail were fused together so the club on the end could be swung.

The tail club of *Tarchia* was made of solid bone. *Tarchia* had big muscles at the base of the tail so it could swing the club with great force. Any meat-eating dinosaur attacking *Tarchia* would be in great danger of having its legs broken by the swinging club.

STYGIMOLOCH

At the end of the Cretaceous Period, a group of dinosaurs called the marginocephalians evolved. One group of marginocephalians was the boneheads. These goat-sized animals had a massive lump of bone on their head that they used as a battering ram. One of the strangest-looking boneheads was *Stygimoloch*.

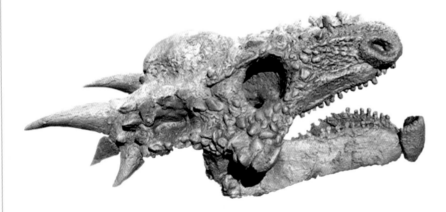

Fossil dinosaur skulls are rare, because the delicate bones fall to pieces soon after death. The skulls of the marginocephalians are different. They were so solid that they are often found as fossils, even though the rest of the skeleton has disappeared.

ANIMAL
FACTFILE

NAME: *Stygimoloch* (horned devil from the river of death)

PRONOUNCED: stig-ih-moe-lock

GROUP: Marginocephalian

WHERE IT LIVED: Canada and the mid-west of the United States

WHEN IT LIVED: Late Cretaceous Period (68 to 65 million years ago)

LENGTH: 9 feet (2.7 meters)

SPECIAL FEATURES: The stiff, straight tail was used for balance

FOOD: Plants

MAIN ENEMY: Big meat-eating dinosaurs like *Tyrannosaurus*

DID YOU KNOW?: All boneheads used their heavy heads as weapons to head-butt their rivals.

Stygimoloch had a spectacular number of horns around its skull. These would have been used to make it look bigger and fiercer than it actually was, to scare away enemies.

TRICERATOPS

Triceratops is one of the most recognizable of the dinosaurs. It had a huge rhinoceros-like body and a massive bony head with three horns pointing forward. It roamed the plains of North America in herds at the very end of the "Age of Dinosaurs."

Triceratops had a big beak at the front of its mouth. It used this to snip off shoots and twigs from bushes and trees. It had chopping teeth at the back of its mouth, and cheek pouches to hold its food while chewing it.

Triceratops was a ceratopsian dinosaur. There were many types of ceratopsian dinosaurs. They all looked very similar to one another, except for the number and arrangement of horns on the head. Some had a single horn on the nose, some had a pair of horns over the eyes, and some had horns on the armored shield around the neck.

ANIMAL
FACTFILE

NAME: *Triceratops* (three-horned face)

PRONOUNCED: try-sair-oh-tops

GROUP: Marginocephalian (ceratopsian group)

WHERE IT LIVED: North America

WHEN IT LIVED: Late Cretaceous Period (72 to 65 million years ago)

LENGTH: 25 feet (7.5 meters)

SPECIAL FEATURES: A solid armored shield around the neck

FOOD: Tough plants

MAIN ENEMY: Big meat-eating dinosaurs like *Tyrannosaurus*

DID YOU KNOW?: *Triceratops* was one of the last dinosaurs to evolve before all dinosaurs became extinct 65 million years ago, leaving only their descendants, the birds.

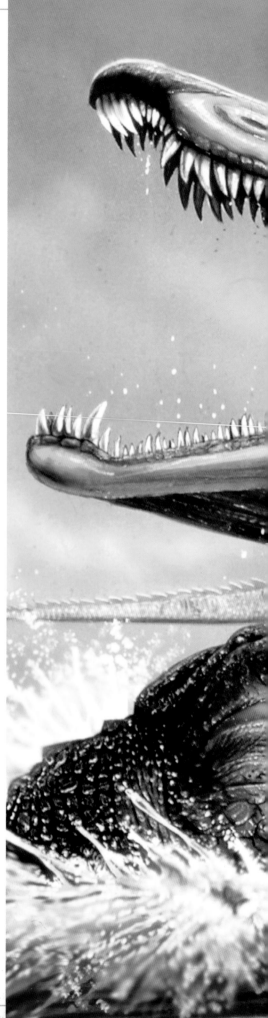

SUCHOMIMUS

This frightening creature belongs to a group of dinosaurs called the spinosaurids. These fish eating creatures lived in the Early Cretaceous Period. *Suchomimus* might have used its claws to hook the fish out of water, throw them onto the land, and snap them up in its long jaws.

Suchomimus was a very powerful dinosaur. Its skull was crocodile-like, with a long snout and a large number of sharp teeth. These would have allowed it to grasp the slippery surface of a fish's scaly skin.

Suchomimus was a fierce predator, but even it was hunted by bigger creatures. In this picture, a gigantic crocodile lunges out of the water to attack *Suchomimus*.

ANIMAL
FACTFILE

NAME: *Suchomimus*
(crocodile mimic)

PRONOUNCED: soo-cho-my-mas

GROUP: Theropod

WHERE IT LIVED: North Africa

WHEN IT LIVED: Early Cretaceous Period (110 to 100 million years ago)

LENGTH: 36 feet (11 meters)

SPECIAL FEATURES: Long narrow crocodile-like jaws

FOOD: Fish

MAIN ENEMY: A gigantic crocodile called *Sarcosuchus*

DID YOU KNOW?: The spinosaurids were a widespread group. Closely related dinosaurs have been found in England, Thailand, and Brazil.

BUITRERAPTOR

Scientists used to think that the small, fast, meat-eating dinosaurs that looked like birds only lived in Europe, Africa, and North America. Then, in 2005, scientists found the remains of *Buitreraptor* in South America. In the Cretaceous Period, South America was an island, like Australia today. This means that the ancestors of *Buitreraptor* and the rest of the bird-like dinosaurs must have existed before the continents broke up, maybe 200 million years ago.

Scientists have not found fossilized feathers with *Buitreraptor*. They think it had feathers because its long legs and light build show that it was very active, and so probably warm-blooded. Most warm-blooded animals have fur or feathers to keep themselves warm. Relatives of *Buitreraptor* had feathers, so it is likely that *Buitreraptor* did, too.

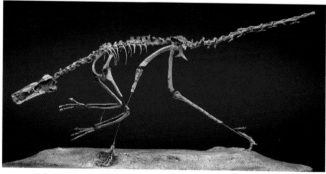

Several skeletons of *Buitreraptor* were found in the same general area, in South America. It looks as though it was quite a common animal at the time. From the many remains, scientists have been able to build up a complete skeleton.

ANIMAL
FACTFILE

NAME: *Buitreraptor* (Vulture hunter)

PRONOUNCED: bewt-re-rap-tor

GROUP: Theropod

WHERE IT LIVED: Argentina

WHEN IT LIVED: Late Cretaceous Period of the Mesozoic Era (90 million years ago)

LENGTH: 4 feet (1.2 meters), but most of this was tail and neck. The body was the size of a chicken.

SPECIAL FEATURES: A bird-like dinosaur with feathers, long legs, wing-like limbs, and a long beak-like snout. It had smaller and fewer teeth than other meat-eating dinosaurs.

FOOD: Small animals

MAIN ENEMY: Bigger meat-eaters

DID YOU KNOW?: The long, narrow jaws and small, widely-spaced teeth may mean that *Buitreraptor* probed down burrows for snakes. Scientists found fossils of snakes at the *Buitreraptor* site.

Deinonychus

Is it a bird? Is it a dinosaur? In the Cretaceous
Period, some of the more active meat-eating
dinosaurs were so bird-like that it is difficult
to decide if they were birds or dinosaurs.
Deinonychus was one of the most bird-like.

Deinonychus
did not fly – its arms were too
small to support its body in flight. It had a
heavy head, toothy jaws, and a long, stiff tail
to balance it as it ran. These are dinosaur
features rather than bird features.

The bones of *Deinonychus* were lightweight and hollow, just like a bird's. It had strong muscles for running or jumping. It was obviously a very active animal, and so it was probably warm-blooded. It is likely that *Deinonychus* had a feathery coat to keep it warm.

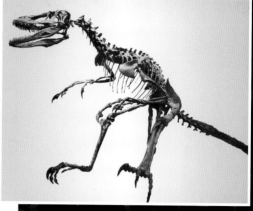

ANIMAL FACTFILE

NAME: *Deinonychus* (terrible claw)

PRONOUNCED: dye-non-ik-us

GROUP: Theropod

WHERE IT LIVED: Western United States

WHEN IT LIVED: Middle Cretaceous Period (110 to 100 million years ago)

LENGTH: 10 feet (3 meters), including the long tail

SPECIAL FEATURES: Big killing claw, 5 inches (12 cm) long, on the hind foot, for slashing its prey

FOOD: Other dinosaurs

MAIN ENEMY: None

DID YOU KNOW?: The fossils of several *Deinonychus* have been found surrounding those of a big plant-eater. They may have hunted this animal in packs.

TYRANNOSAURUS

Since its discovery about a hundred years ago, *Tyrannosaurus* has been regarded as one of the fiercest dinosaurs that ever lived. Weighing over six tons, *Tyrannosaurus* would have been an unstoppable force once it began to attack.

Tyrannosaurus was a fearsome hunter. The remains of duckbilled dinosaurs have been found with chunks torn out of them – in the exact shape of *Tyrannosaurus'* mouth. Fossilized *Tyrannosaurus* dung has been found, full of crunched-up bone fragments from the biggest plant-eaters of the time.

Tyrannosaurus walked on two legs with its back horizontal. Its massive jaws and killing teeth were thrust forward, and its body was balanced by a heavy tail. This is how *Tyrannosaurus* moved about and became the terror of the last dinosaurs that ever existed.

ANIMAL FACTFILE

NAME: *Tyrannosaurus* (tyrant lizard)

PRONOUNCED: tie-ran-oh-sawr-us

GROUP: Theropod

WHERE IT LIVED: Canada and the Western United States

WHEN IT LIVED: Late Cretaceous Period (85 to 65 million years ago)

LENGTH: 40 feet (12 meters)

SPECIAL FEATURES: Huge head with forward pointing eyes to help in hunting, and tiny arms

FOOD: Other dinosaurs — especially duckbills

MAIN ENEMY: None

DID YOU KNOW?: It's possible that *Tyrannosaurus* was a scavenger as well as a hunter.

ANIMAL FAMILIES GLOSSARY

Ammonite — a group of sea-living cephalopods common in the seas of dinosaur times. They were like squid but in coiled shells, and the shells of each species were all quite different from one another. Many can be found as fossils today.

Cephalopod — literally the "head-footed" animals. The modern types, the octopus and squid, appear to have legs branching from their faces. In prehistoric times many of them had chambered shells.

Ichthyosaur — a group of sea-going reptiles. They were well-adapted to living in the sea and looked like dolphins or sharks. They had fins on the tail and back, and paddles for limbs. Ichthyosaurs were common in the Triassic and the Jurassic Periods, but died out in the Cretaceous.

Marginocephalian — the plant-eating dinosaur group that had ornamented heads. The ornaments were sometimes horns and neck shields, and sometimes were domes of bone used as battering rams.

Mosasaur — a group of sea reptiles from the Late Cretaceous Period. They were very much like swimming lizards with paddles instead of feet. Indeed they were very closely related to the monitor lizards of today.

Ornithopod — the plant-eating dinosaur group that usually went about on two legs. They were present throughout the Late Triassic and Jurassic Periods but it was in the later Cretaceous Period that they became really important.

Plesiosaur — the group of swimming reptiles with paddle-shaped limbs and flat bodies. There were two types — the long-necked type and the whale-like, short-necked type. They lived throughout dinosaur times.

Pterosaur — the flying reptiles of the age of dinosaurs. They had broad leathery wings supported on a long fourth finger, and were covered in hair to keep them warm.

Spinosaurid — a type of theropod dinosaur.

Theropod — the meat-eating dinosaur group. They all had the same shape: long jaws with sharp teeth, strong hind legs, smaller front legs with clawed hands, and a small body balanced by a long tail.

Thyreophoran — the armored dinosaur group. There were two main lines. The first to develop were the plated stegosaurs, and later came the armor-covered ankylosaurs.

GLOSSARY

Adapted — changed to survive in a particular habitat or weather conditions.

Ancestors — an early form of the animal group that lived in the past.

Carnivore — a meat-eating animal.

Carrion — the meat left over from a dead animal.

Ceratopsian dinosaur — a type of dinosaur that had frills, spikes, and horns as protection.

Cold-blooded — animals, such as reptiles or amphibians, which rely on their environment to control their body temperature.

Conifer — an evergreen tree such as a fir or pine.

Continents — the world's main land masses, such as Africa and Europe.

Duckbills — a type of dinosaur that had a beak that looked like a duck's beak or bill.

Evolution — changes or developments that happen to all forms of life, over millions of years, as a result of changes in the environment.

Evolve — to change or develop.

Extinct — an animal group which no longer exists.

Flexible — able to twist and turn easily.

Fossils — the remains of a prehistoric plant or animal that have been buried for a long time and become hardened in rock.

Open plains — wide spaces without trees.

Ornithopod — a type of plant-eating dinosaur.

Plesiosaurs — reptiles that lived in the sea.

Prehistory — a time before humans evolved.

Prey — animals that are hunted by other animals as food.

Primitive — a very early stage in the development of a species.

Reptiles — cold-blooded, crawling, or creeping animals with a backbone.

Scavenger — an animal that feeds off food other animals have hunted.

Snout — an animal's nose.

Soared — flew high in the sky.

Streamlined — a smooth, bullet-shaped body that makes it easy for the animal to move through the air or water.

Vertebrae — small bones that form the spine.

Wingspan — the length of a bird's wings, from the tip of one to the tip of the other.

INDEX

PICTURE CREDITS

T = top, B = bottom, R = right, L = left

Main image: 10-11, 20-21 Simon Mendez;
6-7, 8-9, 12-13, 14-15, 16-17, 18-19, 22-23, 24-25, 26-27, 28-29 Luis Rey

42TL, 4TR, 5 (Cenozoic Era), 7, 9, 11, 18, 21, 22, 29 Ticktock Media archive;
5 (Mesozoic Era top, Paleozoic Era top) Simon Mendez; 5 (Mesozoic Era center, Paleozoic Era bottom) Luis Rey;
5 (Mesozoic Era bottom) Lisa Alderson; 15 Chris Tomlin; 13, 16 Gondwana Studios; 25 The Field Museum

Every effort has been made to trace the copyright holders and we apologize in advance for any unintentional omissions.
We would be pleased to insert the appropriate acknowledgment in any subsequent edition of this publication.